3.40

The Discovery Books are prepared

under the educational supervision of

Mary C. Austin, Ed.D.

Reading Specialist and

Professor of Education

Western Reserve University

A DISCOVERY BOOK

GARRARD PUBLISHING COMPANY
CHAMPAIGN, ILLINOIS

George W. Goethals

Panama Canal Engineer

by Jean Lee Latham

illustrated by Hamilton Greene

Contents

George W. Goethals: Panama Canal Engineer

CHAPTER

Chapter *1*

The Parade

"Georgie!" Mother called. "Do you want to see the parade?"

If only his mother would not call him "Georgie"! It was all right to call a little boy that. But he was seven.

"Coming!" he yelled.

He raced into the kitchen. He washed his face and hands in the wash pan on the shelf.

Soon he was trotting down the street with Father and Johnny. He had to trot to keep up.

Johnny was nine and tall for his age. George wished he could be nine right now too.

Then maybe Mother would not call him "Georgie." His name was George Washington Goethals, he thought. No boy named George Washington ought to be called "Georgie"!

What a grand parade this would be! Ever since George could remember, the Civil War had been going on. Now it was over. Every week or two, more boys came home to Brooklyn. People always came out to cheer and wave at their heroes.

Father stopped. "Here is a good place. You boys stand close to the street. I'll stand back here. I can see over people's heads."

George heard the *rat-a-tat-tat* of the drums, then the *thump-a-thump* of feet. He took a deep breath. Someday he would be marching like that!

He was named for a soldier. He was George Washington Goethals.

A woman said, "Oh, look at that beautiful baby! With his blue eyes and yellow curls!"

George looked around to see the baby. The woman was pointing at him.

He ducked his head. He worked his way through the crowd. He began to run.

He ran and ran. He stopped to rest. He ran again. He ought to be home by now. Had he run the wrong way?

He spoke to a policeman. He told him where he lived.

The policeman pointed. "That way, lad. But it's a long, long walk. Think you can make it?"

"Yes, sir. Thank you, sir. I'll just keep on going till I get there."

Before George got home, he saw his father coming.

"Father!" He began to run again.

Father hugged him. "What happened?"

"A woman called me a 'beautiful baby.' *A baby!*"

"I know, son. I know just how it feels."

"No, you don't! Not as big as you are. Nobody could call you a baby."

"But they did when I was your size, especially women." Father spoke in a high, squeaky voice. " 'Oh, look at that beautiful baby!' "

George giggled. He felt better. He said, "I was so mad I got turned around. I ran the wrong way. So I asked a policeman to make sure I was right. Then I just kept on."

Father patted his shoulder. "Spoken like a man! I never heard better advice. Not even from a man ten feet tall."

George giggled again. Father was fun!

"Yes, sir, George! You stick to that! Make sure you're right. Then just keep on!"

Chapter *2*

"Not in Father's
Footsteps"

Big news came one night when George was eleven. Father said, "How would you children like to move across East River to New York City?"

John said, "Fine!"

Annie was only nine. She said, "Oh, no! I'd miss my friends!"

"You'll find more friends, dear," Mother said. "Friends are everywhere."

Father said, "There's lots more work for a carpenter in New York. George, what do you think of moving?"

George was thinking, "New York City is big. No one will look at me there. Nobody will say, 'Oh, what a beautiful child!'" But he said, "I think there will be lots to see."

There was lots to see, and lots to smell too. George could walk along the docks and sniff. He could smell salt water and tar and spices and fish. He could go to the shop where Father and other carpenters worked and smell the wood. Cedar wood smelled best.

"Are you going to follow in your father's footsteps?" a man asked him.

"No," Father said. "George will be something important. A doctor or a lawyer or something like that."

"It'll take a lot of money," the man said. "More than you'll ever have."

"I'll help earn money!" George thought. "I'll start now. I'll keep on and keep on until I have enough."

He had seen boys running along the streets. They carried messages. He could do that too.

Two weeks later George raced down the hall and into his schoolroom.

The teacher said, "Late again! Two times in two weeks!" She wrote a note. "Take this to the principal!"

"Yes, ma'am." George went down the hall to the principal's office. His knees were shaking.

Mr. Beers looked up and smiled. "Yes, George?" He read the note. He was not smiling now. But he did not frown, either. "Sit down, George."

"Yes, sir."

"It isn't like you to be late. Why? Tell me about it. What's the trouble?"

"I was running messages, sir. The places were farther than I thought."

"Why are you running messages?"

"So I won't follow in my father's footsteps."

"What!"

"He wants me to be a doctor or a lawyer or something. But it will take a lot of money."

"I see." Mr. Beers wrote a note. "Take this to your teacher."

"Yes, sir."

"And suppose you just run messages *after* school?"

"Yes, sir. Is that all, sir?"

"One other thing." Mr. Beers held out his hand. "Good luck, George."

18

"Thank you, sir!" George marched out of the office, smiling. Mr. Beers was a wonderful man!

Just before George was fifteen a teacher said one day, "George, you are wanted in Mr. Beers's office."

"Yes, ma'am."

George went slowly down the hall. What in the world had he done?

Chapter *3*

"You Will Not Graduate!"

Mr. Beers was smiling. "George, you are graduating soon, aren't you?"

"Yes, sir."

"What are you going to do?"

"Go to City College, sir. Then I'll go on and study how to be a doctor or a lawyer or something."

"Do you have enough money?"

"No, sir. But I have enough money to start."

"You'll be working and going to school too?"

"Yes, sir."

"City College has the name of being a mighty stiff school. To work and go to school both is going to be hard. Well, good luck!"

"Thank you, sir!"

By the spring of 1876, George was glad that he would soon be through City College. It *had* been hard work.

He had done everything from running messages to addressing envelopes to earn money.

One night he addressed five hundred envelopes. He looked at the clock. It was after ten, and he still had five hours of studying to do. He would have to get up at six. He leaned his head on his hands a minute and closed his eyes to rest them.

A hand on his shoulder wakened him. "Georgie! Did you study all night?"

He jumped up and stared at the clock. "No! I went to sleep! I haven't done my lesson! I'm going to be late!"

He doused cold water on his face and ran his fingers through his hair.

"George, you can't keep on this way! You'll make yourself sick!"

He kissed his mother, picked up his books, and ran from the room.

Class was half over when he got there.

The teacher said, "Don't bother to sit down, Mr. Goethals. You are wanted in President Webb's office."

What a time to have to see President Webb! He needed a shave and a clean shirt.

He entered President Webb's office and stared. "Mr. Beers!"

"Sit down, Mr. Goethals," President Webb said. "Mr. Beers wants to talk to you."

"Yes, sir."

"Would you like to study for a career free of charge?" Mr. Beers asked. "You would even be paid while you learned."

"Where, sir?"

"At West Point. The army officers there are trained to do more than fight. Army engineers help build our country. They build bridges, roads, railroads, and dams. They build canals and locks to tame our rivers."

"I had never thought of being an engineer," George said, "but I do like mathematics."

"There is an opening at West Point," Mr. Beers said. "A boy failed in his examinations. Our Congressman Cox can pick another boy to take his place."

Examinations! Would he have to take examinations *today?* He knew that he was too tired to think.

"I showed Mr. Cox your grades, both school and college," Mr. Beers said. "You may enter West Point without taking examinations—*on one condition.*"

"What is that, sir?"

"I had to promise Mr. Cox that you would graduate. I told him you had a habit of finishing what you set out to do."

"There is one thing you won't finish," President Webb said. "City College."

"Why not, sir?"

"The Centennial Exposition opens in Philadelphia this summer. It celebrates the hundredth birthday of the United States. West Point wants to have a new crop of cadets ready to show off by then. So you will be entering West Point in April. Well, will you go?"

"Yes, sir!"

The Fourth of July, 1876, George was marching with the other West Point cadets in Philadelphia. Left, right, left, right, they marched in perfect time.

"Someday," he thought, "I may be marching with heroes, coming home from battle!"

Chapter *4*

"Build That Bridge!"

Some of the cadets at the Exposition were ready to rest when they were done marching. But George walked through the crowds in his free time. The biggest crowds were always looking at Mr. Bell's telephone.

People could talk from one room to another through it. Someday, Mr. Bell declared, they would even talk from one house to another!

"I'm glad the telephone didn't happen sooner," George thought. "My legs wouldn't be so strong!"

In 1880 George graduated from West Point, second in a class of 52. He was now a second lieutenant in the Army Engineers. If his country went to war, he would fight for her.

Now, he would help build his country. He had learned a lot, and he knew he would learn more, working under the top men of the Army Engineers.

In 1882 he went clear across the country to an army post at Vancouver, Washington. It took six days by train.

"You think that is a long time?" a navy man said. "It took our ship three months. We had to sail around Cape Horn. The French are digging a canal across Panama. When it is done our journey won't be half so long. I wish they'd hurry and finish it!"

"I wish I could watch them working," George thought. "I'd like to meet the engineers who are building the canal!"

"Well, Mr. Goethals," his captain said one day, "what do you think of our mountains out here?"

"They make me feel small, sir."

"You'd better get over that feeling. It takes a big man to tame mountains, to cut roads out of a mountainside, to build bridges over rivers. Did you ever build a bridge, Mr. Goethals?"

"No, sir."

"You probably will. We always have one to build. They get washed out."

"If I ever do work on building a bridge," George thought, "I hope I am working under a good man!"

One day a colonel sent for George. "Our Spokane River Bridge is washed out. We need it. Fast!"

"What am I supposed to do about it?" George thought. He said, "Yes, sir?"

"Go up and check on things. By the time you are ready to start work we'll have a crew of men there. They will follow your orders."

"*My orders?*" George thought wildly. "How can I give orders about building a bridge?" He said, "Yes, sir!"

He went to pack. His pack mule had a heavy load. George had every book he could find on bridge building.

Chapter *5*

Effie

George had never worked so hard in his life. He read books until the men got there. He was ready to give a few orders.

Then he read half the night to be ready to give orders the next day.

But he built the bridge!

When he got back to Vancouver his friend, young Sam Rodman, hailed him. "George! Will you come and have supper with us?"

"George said, "Fine!"

"My sister is here for a visit."

Girls! But he could not refuse to go now. George groaned inside. He smiled outside. He went to meet Sam's sister.

Effie Rodman had a good handshake and a nice smile. And she didn't say, "Ooo!" She said, "That must have been a job!"

"It was." George drew pictures. He told her all about it. The next night he saw her again.

One night he said, "An army man's wife has a hard life. She never knows where she will live. The Army gives orders. The man has to go. His wife has to leave all her friends."

"There are friends everywhere."

George grinned. "That's exactly what my mother said once!" Funny! He was enjoying talking to a girl.

On Effie's last night she promised to marry George. The next day she set out on her long trip to Massachusetts. They both hoped George's next post would not be so far from Massachusetts.

In September of 1884, he wrote, "Good news! I'm ordered to Ohio, assistant to Colonel William E. Merrill. I'm lucky. They call him 'the tamer of rivers.' He is a past master at canals, locks, bridges, dams and even railroad tracks! And think how much nearer I'll be to Massachusetts! We can set the date for our wedding the first time I can get leave!"

Effie wrote, "I'll be so proud to be wife of the Assistant to a Colonel! I'll keep every blessed button shining on your uniforms!"

Effie's letter was waiting for George when he got to Cincinnati. He smiled over it, shined his own buttons and went to meet Colonel Merrill.

He saluted. "Lieutenant Goethals reporting for duty, sir!"

Colonel Merrill looked him up and down. "Very nice," he said. "Very, *very* nice. Nice salute, Mr. Goethals. And a very fine uniform. Do you want my advice, Mr. Goethals?"

"Yes, sir!"

"You'll take off that uniform. You'll pack it away."

Chapter 6

"Overall Days"

George stared at Colonel Merrill. Was the man joking? Telling a West Point man to take off his uniform?

"Yes," Colonel Merrill said, "you'll take off that uniform. You'll put on overalls. You'll start at the bottom. You'll take orders. You'll learn every job from the ground up." He smiled. "My boy, there is a lot to learn. I want you to know everything. Every tool!"

They shook hands on it.

George wrote Effie of his "overall days" under Colonel Merrill.

The Army Engineers had the job of taming rivers. One important thing was to prevent floods. The engineers built dams to hold back a sudden rise of water. They built dikes or levees, which are artificial riverbanks, high enough to keep the rivers from overflowing.

"My 'overall days' are teaching me things I could never learn from books," he wrote.

George did not put on his uniform again until he went to Massachusetts to be married. After the wedding he and Effie came to Ohio.

"I'll show you the most interesting work we are doing," he said. "I'll show you how we sail a ship downstairs."

He drew pictures to explain. "Here is a waterfall in a river. A boat can't go downriver over the falls.

"We dig a big ditch, or canal, to take the boat around the falls. We have an upper canal, above the falls, and a lower canal, below the falls. We connect the upper and lower canals with locks.

"A lock is a big, watertight box. The sides of the lock are solid. But the upper and lower ends are made of gates that can open and shut.

"Suppose we want to send a ship down past the waterfall. We close both gates of the lock. We run water into the lock until the water is level with the water in the upper canal. We open the upper gates and sail the ship into the lock. We let the water out of the lock until it is level with the water in the lower canal. We open the lower gate. The ship sails into the lower canal. It sails back into the river. It has gone downstairs, around the falls.

"When a ship is coming up the river, we do it just the other way. We sail it into the lock, shut the gates, and raise the water until the ship is high enough to sail into the upper canal."

"By the time you get done here," Effie said, "you'll be able to build the Panama Canal by yourself!"

George hugged her. "I know now what wives are for! They are to help husbands feel important!"

"You are! And you could build that canal lots faster than the French!"

Early in 1889 they heard sad news

about the Panama Canal. The French Company had failed. It owed more money than it could pay. The French still had permission to build the canal, but unless they could raise millions of dollars, they could never do it.

"I wonder what happened?" George said.

"I know!" Effie declared. "Their head men did not have enough 'overall days!' "

In 1891 George's "overall days" were done. He was through taking orders. He was sent to Florence, Alabama, to take charge of work on the Tennessee River, to build a canal and locks.

"I'm shocking the old-timers," he said one day.

"How?" Effie asked.

"I'm going to 'send ships upstairs'

with one lock instead of two. The old-timers are really fuming. Just because nobody has ever tried to lift a ship twenty-six feet with one lock."

"Twenty-six feet! That's higher than a two-story house! Do you think it will work?"

"I *know* it will." He smiled. "I learned this business from the ground up!"

Chapter 7

"Finish the Job!"

George built one lock instead of two. It worked. Men came from all around to see it.

"I'm a lucky man!" he said one day. He was Captain Goethals now. He and Effie had two little sons. George was five and Tommy was a baby.

"I wonder what you'll be doing next?" Effie said.

"Something interesting!" George said. "There are always more rivers to tame!"

But the War Department ordered him to Washington, D.C. They needed brains like his, they said. He sat at a desk. He read reports about jobs going on all over the country.

He wrote notes on the reports. Men should do this, or do that. Men should change this, or change that.

The War Department said, "Fine!"

George muttered. He didn't want to give advice about jobs. He wanted to get out there and do them!

In 1898 the Spanish-American War began.

"They won't keep me on a desk now!" he said. "I'll get to fight!" It had been almost 20 years since he entered West Point. He had never been in a battle yet.

General Brooke asked for George. Another general asked for him too. But George picked General Brooke. He was a fighter.

General Brooke said, "Fine! I need a good water supply in one of our training camps up in Georgia. You are just the man to do the job!"

At last George did get to sail with General Brooke to Puerto Rico. The day came when George was leading his regiment up to the battle line.

He saw a man come riding up to General Brooke, waving a letter. "Important message, sir!"

General Brooke opened the letter.

In a few minutes the men were shouting and throwing their caps in the air. The war was over!

48

For years the French Canal Company had been trying to raise the money to go on building the Panama Canal. But they could not. They sold their rights to build the canal to the United States.

Panama let the United States have a strip of land across their little country from the Atlantic to the Pacific. By 1904 the United States was getting ready to go ahead with the Panama Canal.

"You'll be the head engineer!" Effie said. "I just know you will!"

But a Mr. John Wallace was made head engineer. George worked at a desk in Washington.

In 1905 Mr. Wallace resigned.

"This time they'll pick you!" Effie said.

But President Theodore Roosevelt sent a Mr. John F. Stevens to Panama. John Stevens was a great railroad builder.

"That's that!" George told Effie. "Mr. Stevens will do the job!"

One night in February of 1907 George got a call to go to the White House.

Effie's eyes got big. "To see the President! Oh, George!"

When George got back from the White House, he looked dazed.

"What's wrong?" she asked.

"We leave for Panama in two weeks!"

"George!"

"John Stevens quit. The President pounded his desk. He said, 'I'll send men to Panama who *can't* quit! The Army Engineers! Goethals, you will go to Panama! You will finish the job!'"

Chapter *8*

"White-Suit Days"

George had a busy two weeks. He worked from dawn to midnight. Between times he had to have some white suits made. He would need them when he was not on the job. It was always summer in Panama.

"Maybe on shipboard," he thought, "I can get a little rest."

Forty Congressmen got on the ship. They were going to Panama to "see about that mess down there." They were full of questions.

What was going on down there? Why had two head engineers quit? We had spent millions on Panama. What did we have to show for it? Maybe it was time to stop. And maybe that was just what we would do. If they didn't vote any more money to carry on the job, it would have to stop.

Mr. Stevens met George and Effie in Panama. He was going to stay for two weeks to show George around.

He showed George a map of what the canal would look like when it was done.

The largest part of the canal would be a big lake, made by damming the Chagres River. On the north end of the lake three pairs of locks would raise and lower the ships to sea level.

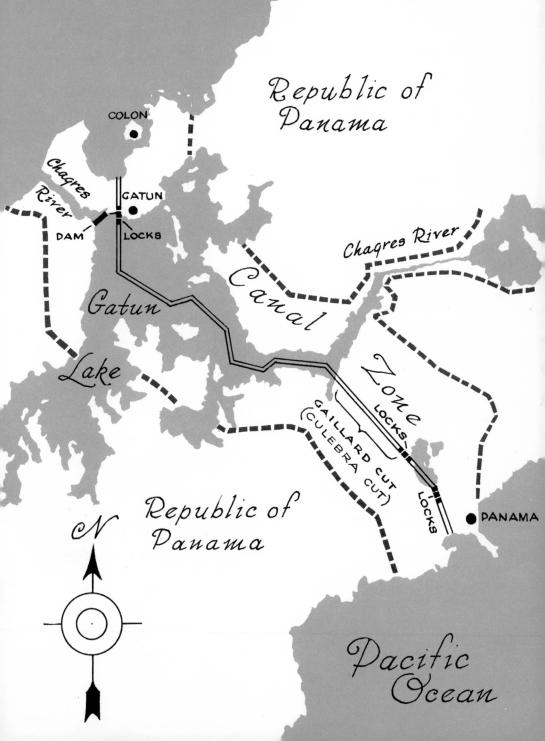

On the south end of the lake would be Culebra Cut, a man-made gorge through nine miles of mountains. Beyond Culebra Cut there would be three more pairs of locks to raise and lower ships to sea level on that end.

Beyond the locks, on each end, deep ship channels were being dug.

The more George saw of the work, the more he admired what Mr. Stevens had done. How could he bear to give it up?

The Congressmen were everywhere. They made remarks. They asked questions. They gave advice.

"I put up with that for two years," Mr. Stevens said. "Idiots trying to tell me how to run my job. I told the President I'd stay till you came. I'd explain things to you. *Then it's yours! All yours!"* He smiled.

But none of the workmen were smiling at George. They would not even look at him if they could help it.

The Canal Zone newspaper had things to say about "military rule." Would the workmen have to march to work? Would they have to stop work to salute when the officers came by?

One night George was to go to a big meeting. Thousands of workers would be there to see their new boss.

When George came in to get ready, Effie had laid out his dress uniform.

But George shook his head. "No more uniforms. Remember my 'overall days'? Then I took off my uniform to learn a job. Now I'll do it to finish a job."

He put on a white suit. He went to the meeting. Men looked at him. They did not make a sound. Mr. Stevens came in. Men stood up and cheered.

The man in charge had read the Canal Zone newspaper. He had a lot of little things to say about "the military." Maybe the men would march to work? He wasn't sure. Maybe Colonel Goethals could tell them how it would be under "the military."

George got up. He looked at the angry faces. These were the men he had to work with. These were the men he needed to finish the job.

He praised the work Mr. Stevens had done. He told the men, "Yes, we are an army. We are fighting together. We

are fighting rivers and mountains to get this job done. Any man who fights a good fight won't have any trouble with 'the military.' "

He sat down. Men clapped. A few of them even smiled.

At the end of March Mr. Stevens went north. George took over. The long job began.

He got up at six. All morning he was out on the job. He must know how all the work was going. Did they need more steam shovels? Did they need more men? How many were sick? Were they getting good food?

All afternoon he worked in his office. After supper he worked again until ten o'clock.

Every Sunday morning he "held court" in his office. Anybody could come to talk to him. A man who bossed 4,000 men could come. A man who shoveled dirt could come.

Sunday afternoon was his only time off. Monday morning, he was up again at six.

"I think I know why those other men quit," Effie said one day. "Two years of this would be about enough."

"It won't be enough to finish the job," George said.

"How long will it take?"

"About ten years."

Chapter 9

The Salute

After two months the workmen did not growl so much about "the military." They were saying things like this:

"That man is fair!"

"He knows his job!"

"He knows every tool in this shop."

"He knows all about railroads."

"He knows locks and canals."

In 1909 George was promoted. He had been a lieutenant colonel. Now he was a full colonel. But he was muttering the morning he heard the news.

More men were down from Washington. He must waste time with them. They wanted to see Culebra Cut. That was the most exciting place now. The great ditch was getting deeper and deeper.

The visitors wanted to go down into the cut. But everything was going wrong. The train stopped time after time. George looked at his watch. It was almost eleven.

The workmen left the ditch at eleven. The dynamiters set off blasts. They tore loose tons of rock and dirt. Nobody could be in the cut then!

The train got to the cut. Exactly eleven o'clock! Dynamite blasts began to go off. Something was wrong. There should have been ten *booms* at a time. There was one *boom,* then silence.

What was wrong?

Boom. Silence. *Boom.* Silence.

Then George began to laugh. The workmen were firing a salute to him!

The workmen waved. They cheered. "Hurrah for the Colonel!"

George waved back. He had a lump in his throat. The men were back of him now, fighting with him. He needed them. It had been a hard job. It was getting harder every day.

The trouble was here at the cut. It was very deep now, and the sides of the mountains were breaking loose. Tons of dirt would break off and slide into the cut. A slide might last only half a day. But it might take the men a month to shovel out the dirt and rocks. Sometimes it took longer.

George had three good men in charge of the different parts of the canal. Colonel Gaillard was at Culebra Cut. Another colonel was at the Atlantic end. Mr. Williamson was at the Pacific end. He was the only head man who was not in the army.

Early in 1913 Mr. Williamson came to George. "I hate to say this. I want to resign—to quit! But our job is almost done. And I have a good job waiting for me in England."

"Then go," George said. "And thank you for all your help."

"Who will take over for me?"

"Don't worry," George said.

He knew he could not get a man who could take Mr. Williamson's place. He would have to take care of it himself.

He was glad his other head men could not quit. But he worried about Colonel Gaillard. The men at Culebra said the colonel was getting "meaner than a snake." George couldn't understand it. Gaillard was one of the most patient men in the world.

Of course, the slides were enough to wear any man out. George could only pray they would not have another one.

One day a man dashed into his office. "Sir! You're wanted at Culebra! Fast! The worst slide yet!"

Chapter *10*

Slides!

George got to Culebra and looked at the mess. It was "the worst slide yet." They would be lucky to shovel it out in six months.

Colonel Gaillard was holding his head and shouting. "What are we going to do? What are we going to do?"

"We'll dig it out," George said.

Colonel Gaillard said that he was sick. George sent him north to see a doctor.

The men said, "Bah! He just lost his nerve! That's all!"

Then they got word from the doctor up north. Colonel Gaillard was dying of a brain tumor. He must have been in pain all those last months of the job.

The workmen said, "We were louses! We said he had lost his nerve. He had more than any of us. They ought to name this place for him!"

Effie said, "The poor man. But George, what *can* you do now?"

"Take over his job too."

"Dear, you can't! You're already working all day and half the night!"

"I'm here to finish the job."

Men fought the big slide for nine months. The biggest steam shovels were not getting anywhere. More dirt kept sliding into the cut.

Men said, "What's the use?"

George said, "We'll change our plan of battle!" He let water into the cut. That turned the dirt into runny mud. He brought up dredges—big boats that could scoop up the mud and squirt it out through hoses.

In March of 1914, George got a double promotion. Congress made him a major general. Nobody fired a salute. They were too busy.

In August of 1914, the first ship went through the canal. It had taken almost two years to clear out the big slide. But what a thrilling day it was at the Panama Canal!

"How are you going to celebrate?" Effie asked.

"I'll sleep twenty-four hours. Then I'll think of something."

The newspapers of the world did not say much about the great day at the Panama Canal. They had other head- lines. World War I had begun.

George stayed for one more year at Panama. He had things to see about. The war meant danger. Guns had to be ready to defend the canal.

Finally he resigned. Even an army man could resign when a job was done. He and Effie went to San Francisco. The Panama-Pacific Exposition was there. It was to celebrate success at Panama.

"You look ten years younger!" Effie said.

"I feel 20 years younger!" he told her happily.

Word came from Panama. Slides! Two slides this time!

Effie said, "Oh, *no!*"

George said, "Start packing, dear. We're on our way. The slides at the cut are calling. You know, I'm glad President Wilson changed the name. I'm glad it's Gaillard Cut now. He deserved that!"

He sent a telegram to Washington. The War Department could forget that he had resigned.

He would take the first ship back to Panama. He would finish the job!

Chapter *11*

"Duty. Honor. Country."

It was late in 1916 before George left Panama for the last time. He had been on the job there for over nine years. But now the job was done.

All the world was praising "Colonel Goethals of Panama—the man who built the Canal!"

George shook his head. "No. We never could have done it without the work of John L. Stevens. The canal is his monument. I only finished the job."

George had not been back in the United States long when America entered World War I.

"Finally!" he thought, "I'll get to serve my country!"

General Pershing was in command of the U. S. Army in Europe.

George wrote him. Could he come to Europe and take charge of the Army engineers?

He waited and waited for Pershing's answer. At last it came. Pershing was sorry, but he had good men in charge of the engineers. He did not think he should change things.

President Wilson sent for George. At last! Maybe he'd get to go to Europe!

The War Department had a big job for George. The government had millions

of men at the front. Somebody must see that they got the supplies they needed. George was just the man for that!

He had never been so disappointed. But he took the job. He stayed on the job till the war ended.

One day in 1918 he stood on a street in New York City. Over 50 years ago he had stood like this on a street in Brooklyn.

The war was over. Heroes were coming home. People were waiting to cheer and wave.

He heard again the *rat-a-tat-tat* of the drums, and the *thump-a-thump* of the marching feet. The crowd cheered. He cheered too. Then he sighed. He was almost 60. And he had never had a chance to fight for his country.

The United States, France and Great Britain all decorated George for what he had done to help win the war.

Many universities, societies and clubs honored him for his work at Panama.

"I've counted up," Effie said once. "Do you know you've won about three dozen honors?"

"All I know," George growled, "is that I am now an ex-soldier who never got to fight for his country."

"George Washington Goethals!" Effie said. "You fought for your country and for the whole world! You fought the battle of the Panama Canal for almost ten years!"

George smiled and kissed her. "Do you remember when I told you what wives are for?"

"Yes!" Effie said. "And you *are* important! There are dozens of big engineering jobs where your brains are needed!"

George sighed. "Yes. I can sit at a desk and plan jobs for other men."

Important as his work was, George never did enjoy desk jobs. But he did enjoy his summers at Martha's Vineyard, a little island off Cape Cod.

Both their boys were married now and had little sons. George and Effie loved to have the little boys spend their summers with them.

The only hard time George had was when a little grandson wanted to hear about "How you were a hero in a war."

"Never," George said. "No parades for me."

In 1928 George died. He was buried with military honors at West Point.

He had never fought in a war, but he had lived up to West Point's motto: "Duty. Honor. Country."

So a riderless horse walked behind his casket. Boots turned backwards in the stirrups said a leader was dead.

Soldiers fired a salute over his grave. A bugler sounded taps.

A soldier had finished his job.